L'ADOLESCENZA E LA NOTTE
ADOLESCENCE AND NIGHT

Luigi Fontanella

Translated by
Giorgio Mobili

Fomite
Burlington, VT

Poems Copyright © 2021   Luigi Fontanella
Translation Copyright © 2021 Giorgio Mobili
Cover image: Francesca R. Pasqualini

All rights reserved. No part of this book may be reproduced in any form or by any means without the prior written consent, except in the case of brief quotations used in reviews and certain other noncommercial uses permitted by copyright law.

ISBN-13: 978-1-953236-02-9
Library of Congress Control Number: 2020945516
Fomite
58 Peru Street
Burlington, VT 05401

*To all my friends,
lost along the way or still near me*

Indice

L'adolescenza   2
La notte   76

Nota   136
Nota sull'autore   140
Nota sul traduttore   142

Contents

Introduction	i
Adolescence	3
Night	77
Author's Note	137
About the Author	141
About the Translator	143

Introduction

Adolescence and Night, winner of the prestigious 2015 Pascoli Prize and Viareggio Jury Prize, revisits what is likely the most quintessential of all modern conundrums: the "search for lost time", a Proustian theme on which Luigi Fontanella has been carrying out for years, both in verse and in prose, his own idiosyncratic meditation. In more than one sense, this collection is the poetic counterpart to Fontanella's 2009 novel *Controfigura*, a narrative shot through with lyrical intensity in the same measure that the poetry of *Adolescence and Night* is interspersed with prosaic interludes. In both works, Fontanella entrusts imagination with the arduous task of wresting the past from its destiny of oblivion, (a past, however – to quote Faulkner – that *"is never dead, it's not even past")*, by revivifying it in the present, through an attitude of openness to its visitations during our day-to-day engagement with life.

In *Adolescence and Night*, the rescued past is that of the early adolescent years that Luigi spent in Salerno, Italy, where he was also born in 1943.

They were bittersweet years of post-war hardship, spent amid neighborhood scuffles, burgeoning sexuality, and the ineffable happiness of soccer matches in "the little field down the street" (the first section of the book, "Adolescence", is fittingly dedicated to François Truffaut). But it was also the foundational moment in which an identity was born, and was clear and stable for a seemingly never-ending instant, before losing itself in the "unbelonging" of adult life ("I never entered life", 19).

The second section of the book ("Night") clarifies how the author's tactic of recovery of the past relies, crucially, on the alliance of night, dream, and poetry. But what can such a triangulation produce? Certainly not the past *tout court*, irrecoverable by definition; but rather, sequences, scenes, shards of memories like film clippings, always the same with marginal (but infinite) variations ("repetitions / repetitions", 109), obsessively reiterated in a vortex of images of which the author is now the self-aware director ("this is a film I can modify / as I please", 51), now the spectator-victim. In other words, Fontanella is well aware that any attempt to retrieve what has been lost, no matter how tenacious, must end in failure; unless it transforms into a demiurgic gesture, which, by means of an operation of montage, *rewrites* what cannot be regained.

Indeed, it is a dangerous undertaking—one in which life itself is at stake. The very moment the poet, with Faustian verve, calls upon the power of Night to preside over his necromancies ("O Night katabasis", 111), he is assailed by fantasies of self-annihilation ("I've always imagined / myself disappearing into nothingness", 49), of dissolution into the undifferentiated chasm of time. It is not irrelevant, then, to find in *Vertigo*, the 1958 Hitchcock masterpiece (explicitly referenced in the poem "The music is the same", 61), one of the formal and ideological centers of *Adolescence and Night*. As is well known, the figure of the vortex (which also dominates this collection) is prominent in *Vertigo*, from the famous spiraling title sequence to the plot itself, which hinges on an original event followed by its darker repetition. At the same time that the repetition exposes the betrayal in the original event, though, it also reveals the truth of love, which transcends every falsehood. Does not the same happen here? Remembering is tantamount to deceiving (oneself and others), to betraying the past. Yet, paradoxically, betrayal is the only possible means by which the past can be approached, in a way that lets a kind of *truth* emerge: in Fontanella, that is the truth of his militant *passion*—in the double sense of love and suffering—for what once was. This passion, which is never more manifest than when the verse modulates into the affectionate naming of real-life companions from the past, is perhaps the only thing that can alleviate, and ultimately redeem, the human sorrow over loss, the anguish in the face of the final abyss where—to quote the very last line of the book—"All talking forbidden. All writing forbidden."

Fontanella avails himself of a terse, vigorous idiom, free of pathetic ostentation yet flexible enough to accommodate suggestive forays into the mysterious sphere of dreams and the unconscious. In my translation, I have sought to adhere fully to this agility of tone as well as to the mercurial rhythms of the original Italian. I feel that Fontanella's poetic writing translates well into English, not only because of its Mediterranean clarity, but also because of its metaphysical thrust, whereby simple quotidian gestures and emotions transcend their geographical-historical specificity to assume universal significance. Through the author's lyrical rendering, the "little concentric kisses", the "straight goal kick", all the "little triumphs or tumbles in the dust" are lifted onto an epic plane, like a bas-relief on an ancient wall, sheltered from the corrosion of time. This, of course, is the mark of true poetry, which ultimately knows no language boundaries. I hope this translation will bring English readers as much joy as it brought me to make it.

> Giorgio Mobili
> California State University, Fresno

I

L'ADOLESCENZA

*Non sei nulla, e sei sempre soltanto
in relazione agli altri, e ciò che tu
sei, lo sei per questa relazione.*
                                Kierkegaard

*... è già notte tarda, e non ho
voglia di dormire; non so cosa mi
manca – e ho già più di vent'anni.*
                                Chopin

I

ADOLESCENCE

> *You are nothing and exist merely in relation to others, and you are what you are in this relation.*
> Kierkegaard

> *…it's already late at night, and I don't feel like sleeping; I don't know what I lack—and I'm already more than twenty years old.*
> Chopin

La mia banda aveva coraggio da vendere
le alleanze già fatte.
Ognuno porta il suo carico, ognuno
bada a se stesso. Parole
sfrenate per meglio rappresentarsi.
Cosa mi resta di quella frenesia?
Il tempo non contava per le nostre mani
Elvira Forte alla finestra avrebbe concesso
il suo sorriso a ogni vincitore.

My gang had courage to spare
the alliances already settled.
Everyone carries his burden, everyone
looks after himself. Wild words
for us to appear in a better light.
What remains of all that frenzy?
Time didn't matter to our hands
Elvira Forte in the window would've granted
her smile to every winner.

Non siamo più qui.
L'odore della stanza scova
i morti che mi furono vicini.
Cosa resta di quella frenesia?
A chi appartiene quello spazio? Le foto
sono rinchiuse in un album obsoleto.

We are no longer here.
The smell of the room dredges up
the dead who were close to me.
What remains of that frenzy?
To whom does this space belong? The photos
are sealed in an obsolete album.

Dopo una giornata afosa
nella penombra meridiana
Anna Pierro della porta accanto
consuma con me i primissimi
ardori, spasimi ignoti
in piccoli baci concentrici.
Nel calendario è segnata una data:
millenovecentocinquantaquattro
29 agosto. Ho quasi undici anni.

After a muggy day
in the noon half-light
Anna Pierro from next door
consummates with me her early
ardors, unknown paroxysms
in little concentric kisses.
There is a date marked on the calendar:
August 29th, nineteen-fifty-four.
I am almost eleven.

Torna un'estate antica. Ragazzi
corrono al lato di un cimitero
tante croci uguali
per chi aveva combattuto
in una guerra straniera. Ora
per sempre giovani
si danno nuovi appuntamenti
bisbigliando sottoterra
nell'estate che non finisce mai
un'estate antica che si nasconde
nel suo culmine estremo.

An ancient summer returns. Boys
run alongside a cemetery
so many identical crosses
for those who had fought
in a foreign war. Now
forever young
they arrange new get-togethers
whispering underground
in the never-ending summer
an ancient summer that hides
in its extreme apex.

Siamo pronti all'assalto.
Voce che rimbalza dal suo orlo.
Arde nel vortice, arde nel vortice che
ha trovato il suo estremo.
Siamo gli ultimi eroi.

Nel precipizio una luce
rotea da un punto all'altro. Smembra i suoni
di ogni parola non detta. Siamo gli ultimi eroi.
Pronti all'assalto.
Nulla è cambiato.

We are poised for attack.
Voice that bounces off its edge.
It burns in the vortex, it burns in the vortex that
has found its end.
We are the last heroes.

Inside the precipice a light
spins from one point to the next. Dismembers the
       sounds
of every unuttered word. We are the last heroes.
Poised for attack.
Nothing has changed.

Già allora questa fretta
che uccide come una pietra
schiacciata sul petto. I sogni
non si spezzano, non possono
spaccarsi così, in una stretta
improvvisa che lascia fuori
gli occhi.

Already back then this haste
that kills like a stone
pressed against your chest. Dreams
don't shatter, they can't
split open like this, in a sudden
grasp that leaves out
the eyes.

Ci si raduna casualmente.
Qualcuno diventa re in un istante. Era
l'attesa, era l'attesa
che riconciliava i volti
dei vinti e vincitori. Ora
li vorrei tutti qui quei miei compagni.
Ora che ogni scialuppa
è partita, che ogni strada
ha riconquistato il suo spazio.
Ora che il vuoto è in qualche foglio
di giornale che vola per le strade.

We gather casually.
Somebody becomes king in an instant. It was
the wait, it was the wait
that reconciled the faces
of winners and losers. Now
I wish all those friends of mine were here.
Now that every lifeboat
has left, that every street
has reclaimed its own space.
Now that emptiness lies in some old newspaper
blowing in the streets.

Non sono mai entrato nella vita.
Mai appartenuto a qualcuno. Storie
che giungevano al termine, al punto
verticale della fine. Ma mi commuovo
per un nonnulla, l'adolescenza
è assoluta ed eterna
è l'unica cosa che resta.

I never entered life.
Never belonged to someone. Stories
that reached an end, their vertical
endpoint. Yet the slightest thing
moves me to tears, adolescence
is absolute and eternal.
It is all that remains.

Lungo una ringhiera
scorrono i nostri ardori
le prodezze di un' ora.
I pomeriggi assolati
liquefanno il nostro cortile.

Ancora adesso non so
dare una spiegazione
a quelle rapide intese degli occhi
alle nostre corse a perdifiato
le dispute improvvise, il pugno
che partiva di scatto.

Along a handrail
run our ardors
an hour's bravery.
The sun-drenched afternoons
liquefy our courtyard.

Even now I would not know
how to explain
those flickers of understanding in our eyes
our breathtaking races
our sudden disputes, the fist
shooting out.

I'll cross it, though it blast me. Stay, illusion!
If thou hast my sound, or use of voice,
Speak to me.

SHAKESPEARE, *Hamlet*

Brucia il tempo e la sua continua
imminenza. Quanto disteso
e sonnolento l'altro che imbrigliava
sillabe e tormenti!
A chi appartiene quella scena?
È un film muto che scivola
negli occhi allo stato selvaggio
di fronte ai torrioni del cavalcavia
per noi simile a un castello
che solo un eroe sarebbe capace
di attraversare, lassù, uno spettro
che io, giovane Amleto,
sono il solo a saper riconoscere.

I'll cross it, though it blast me. Stay, illusion!
If thou hast my sound, or use of voice,
Speak to me.

                            SHAKESPEARE, *Hamlet*

Time burns through its constant
imminence. How recumbent
and sleepy that other one, as he intertwined
syllables and torments!
To whom does that scene belong?
It's a silent film that slides
into the eyes in the wild state
in front of the overpass towers
that looked to us like a castle
only a hero would be capable
of crossing, up there on top, a ghost
that only I, young Hamlet,
am able to recognize.

Ripeti il tuo numero, vola
da una stanza all'altra.
Non c'è giudice
che dà voti o pagelle
bisogna strappare le pagine.
Ripeti il tuo numero.
Bisogna strappare le pagine:
quelle che mi sono state assegnate.
Non ricordo più che fine abbia fatto:
quel libro non mi è mai appartenuto.

Repeat your number, fly
from one room to the next.
There is no judge
giving out grades or report cards
you need to rip out the pages.
Repeat your number.
You need to rip out the pages:
the ones that were assigned to me.
I don't remember what became of it:
that book never belonged to me.

A occhi socchiusi scorrono
vilipendi e ferite. La sfida
è per chi ci precede. Oppure
làsciati andare:
la nebula mente
soffia un breve respiro.

Affronts and bruises stream
before half-closed eyes. The challenge
is for those who precede us. Or else
let yourself go:
the nebulous mind
blows a short breath.

Avrai i tuoi anni
le tue disgrazie le tue diaspore
le tue speranze.
Dovrai saper riconoscere
il punto in cui incontrerai
l'altro te stesso. Poche
le volte in cui questo avverrà.
Le fermate saranno più
corte e più fervide.

You will have your years
your tragedies your diasporas
your hopes.
You must learn to recognize
the point at which you will meet
your other self. This
will happen but rarely.
The stops will be shorter
and more fervid.

C'è solo da percorrere
lo spazio. La vita trasmessa
abbraccia la distanza.
Resta il segno dei visi
il sorriso di quel ragazzo
che sono stato.
Avremmo potuto giocare un'altra
gara... Renata Ferri al Tito Lucrezio Caro
saliva le scale danzando.
Quel mondo risorge
come una partita di calcio
sul nostro campetto sotto casa
il sudore incolla foglie e capelli, mentre
i maschi corrono a perdifiato.
Il tempo è in quel concentrato assoluto,
fermo e preciso, come
il tiro secco in porta.

You only need to cover
the space. The bequeathed life
embraces the distance.
Only the imprint of the faces
remains, the smile of that boy
I once was.
We could have played another
contest... Renata Ferri at the Tito Lucrezio Caro
dancing up the stairs.
That world is resurrected
like a soccer match
in the little field down the street
sweat glues hair and leaves, while
the boys run at breathtaking speed.
Time is in that absolute concentrate,
still and precise, like
a straight goal kick.

Ricompare improvvisamente
la messinscena di qualche famiglia.
Una la riconosco benissimo.
Ci contiamo nei piatti. Fuori piove.
In certe Domeniche lente e lunghe
io m'attardo a osservare
le gocce d'acqua ai vetri
una pioggia che si ripete
all'infinito, ogni volta,
nel mio percorso a ritroso.

The mise-en-scene of some family
suddenly materializes. I recognize
one of them very well.
We count each other in the plates.
It's raining outside.
On certain slow, long Sundays
I linger to observe
the raindrops on the window panes
a rain that repeats itself
endlessly, every time,
on my journey backwards.

I miei alleati mi attendono nell'ombra.
Li ho aspettati con fiducia e simpatia.
Ho anche pregato per loro. Adesso
i minuti scorrono senza ragione.
Dalla foto che mi è davanti,
ferma nel tempo,
si staccano le persone che vi sono dentro.
Sono diventato uno dei loro volti.
Organizzo le corse nel cortile
do cinque metri di vantaggio a Valerio Sardella
il mio avversario, il mio piccolo Nestore.

My allies await me in the shadows.
I have waited for them with trust and sympathy.
I have even prayed for them. Now
the minutes go by for no reason.
From the picture in front of me,
motionless in time,
the people are jumping out.
I have become one of their faces.
I organize the races in the courtyard
give Valerio Sardella a five-meter advantage
my adversary, my little Nestor.

Cosa voglio di più? Già allora
non mi basta l'offerta quotidiana:
è ancora qui nella mia stanza. Cosa
voglio di più? Voci e ninnoli
si prodigano per una loro presenza,
una loro plausibilità.
Un bambino a un tratto si sveglia e
piange il suo essere venuto al mondo.

What more do I want? Already back then
the day-to-day fare isn't enough for me:
it is still here in my room. What
more do I want? Voices and trinkets
fall over themselves to be present,
to be still plausible.
A child awakens suddenly and
cries over having been born.

Vola, ragazzo, vola.
Non temere lo scatto
di qualche coetaneo più baldanzoso.
Ancora non mi rendo conto
dei grandi problemi, non ho
una cartella. Porto i miei libri
legati a un elastico. Poco fa
Aldo Stella mi è ritornato davanti agli occhi.

Fly, boy, fly.
Do not fear the sprint
of a more audacious peer.
I still have no grasp
of the big issues, I do not own
a briefcase. I still carry my books
strapped by a rubber band. Only minutes ago
Aldo Stella reappeared before my eyes.

La stanza è bianchissima…
non so quale della mia vecchia casa
io mi ci vedo rinchiuso. Sono
nel mio letto con in mano una tazza di caffelatte
nella quale continuo a lavorare con un cucchiaino
traendone lo zucchero. La luce
è sempre più abbacinante
immensa
dilaga in tutta la stanza
(che il sole passi attraverso le pareti?).
Berto nel suo letto accanto al mio
sta sorbendo il suo caffè
il naso nella tazza.
"Mi presti il tuo cucchiaio?"
"Sì se mi dai un po' del tuo zucchero."
"Vergogna! *Strozzino!*", urla
mia madre dall'altra stanza… Non capisco
quella parola, ma di colpo spavento e vergogna
mi ributtano nel presente. Nel sogno
vorrei controbatterla, ma
Berto, mia madre ed io – così come eravamo –
scompariamo ripiombando nell'abisso.

The room is bone-white...
I forget which room of my old house
I see myself cooped up in it. I lie
in my bed holding a cup of caffelatte
that I continue to work on with my spoon
collecting all the sugar. The light
is more and more blinding
immense
it floods the entire room
(is sunlight seeping through the walls?).
Berto in his bed next to mine
is sipping his coffee
nose buried in the cup.
"Can I borrow your spoon?"
"If you let me have some of your sugar."
"Shame on you! *Loan shark*!", yells
my mother from the other room... I don't understand
that word, but at once fright and shame
jolt me back into the present. In my dream
I'd like to offer a rebuttal, but
Berto, my mother and I—just as we were—
have disappeared back into the abyss.

Ci fanno l'appello. Uno per uno
ogni mattina, consegnati
in una colonia estiva
in piena campagna. Un ragazzo
baratta il proprio corpo
per cinque lire nel bagno.
Siamo figli di un dio secondario.
Nessuno ci difenderà,
nessuno forse veramente ci ama.

They take attendance. One by one
every morning, handed over
to a summer camp
deep in the countryside. In the lavatory
a boy trades his body
for five *lire*.
We are the children of a lesser god.
No one will defend us,
perhaps no one really loves us.

Lasciamo i papaveri dove sono,
là dove li vidi la prima volta
cinquant'anni fa. Un amichetto
mi mostra la piccola stella
impressa sulla pelle
al centro del fiore.
Mi emancipo, salto di posto.
Il nostro cortile è un campo di battaglia
piccoli trionfi o cadute nella polvere
fra Tonino Iannone e Franco Arpino.
Bisogna sbrigarsi a crescere.

Let's leave the poppies where they are,
where I first saw them
fifty years ago. A friend
shows me the little star
imprinted on his skin
at the flower's center.
I emancipate myself, change my spot.
Our courtyard is a battlefield
little triumphs or tumbles in the dust
between Tonino Iannone and Franco Arpino.
We must hurry and grow up.

Non mi sarei mai immaginato qui.
Ancora adesso mi è difficile
associarmi ai sorrisi, alle strette di mano,
i brindisi, i convenevoli d'uso.
Le conversazioni non fanno per me.
Parlo con la voce d'un altro
gesti e sguardi segnalano
altri campi. Stasera New York è
un imbuto grandioso.

I never pictured myself here.
Even now it's hard for me
to associate myself to the smiles, the handshakes,
the toasts, the usual pleasantries.
I am not one for conversation.
I speak with someone else's voice
gestures and looks signal
other networks. Tonight New York is
a majestic funnel.

Rischiamo un'avventura continua
o uno stacco imperioso, improvviso.
La paura si mescola con l'eccitazione.
Devo completarmi
in un avventore ignoto
prima che il silenzio mi sprofondi
nel suo respiro. Ho sempre
immaginato di scomparire nel vuoto.

We risk a constant adventure
or a sudden, imperious break.
Fear mixes with excitement.
I have to complete myself
into an unknown customer
before silence drowns me
in its breath. I've always imagined
myself disappearing into nothingness.

Partire da una macchia
per continuare in un disegno
di senso compiuto. Ora
un volto obliquo, poi
un stradina soleggiata.
La regia della mensa
allinea visi e mani
che sanno destreggiarsi nel buio.
Questo è un film che posso modificare
a mio piacimento.

You start with a stain
then develop it into a meaningful
drawing. Now an oblique face, now
a sunny street.
The stage direction of the cafeteria
aligns faces and hands
that know how to get by in the dark.
This is a film I can modify
as I please.

Eccomi in un ritratto con mio fratello Berto:
due ragazzi allo sbaraglio.
Salta il clic della serratura
l'inquilino è un giovane sorridente.
Non sappiamo nulla di noi due.
Mondi separati da un metro di spazio
che raramente s'incrociano. Questo
il grande vantaggio. Questa
l'irreparabile perdita.

Here I am in a portrait with my brother Berto:
two boys adrift.
The door lock clicks open
the tenant is a smiling young man.
We know nothing about each other.
Worlds separated by a one-meter gap
hardly ever crossing each other. This
is the big advantage. This
is the irreparable loss.

Il pomeriggio se ne va nel filo
d'un desiderio continuo.
Conosci quest'ora. Ragazzo,
cercavi i compagni giusti,
il prodigio di un pugno
tirato a caso. Tu conosci quest'ora.
In una buca scavata
nel campetto vicino casa
figure di sogni proibiti:
i primi desideri,
il seme sprecato più volte.

The afternoon winds down on the thread
of a constant desire.
You know this hour. Boy,
you sought the right companions,
the wonder of a punch
pulled at random. You know this hour.
In a hole dug in the little
field down the street
figures of forbidden dreams:
the first desires,
the oft-wasted seed.

Si preparava la scenografia
del futuro. Il principio era questo:
un momento e già subito un ammasso di anni...
Oggetti accumulati che col tempo
perdono ogni precisa identità
ogni significato. Rivivono
in occhiate notturne
prima di andare a letto
solo di passaggio solo di passaggio
appena fissati per un attimo
e già rientrati in se stessi.
Scenografia che andrebbe scompigliata.
Dovrei disfarmene, distruggerla.
Mi sopravvivrà
chissà in quale altro spazio
chissà per quali altri immemori occhi.

The choreography of the future
was being prepared. The principle was this:
an instant, and in a flash already a heap of years...
Accumulated objects that over time
lose all definite identity
all significance. They live again
in our nighttime glances
before we go to bed
only in transit only in transit
fixed for barely an instant in time
and already retreated into themselves.
A choreography that should be disarranged.
I should get rid of it, destroy it.
It will survive me
in who knows what other space
for whose oblivious eyes.

Lasciti estremi in un
circolare concerto. Voci sillabe
rimbalzano affollate.
Ritornano a me:
un brusìo infinito da cui estraggo
solo qualche scoria
appena appagante. Sento soltanto
il respiro che accompagna
il resto del mio camminare.
Cos'è che potrebbe veramente appagarmi?
Non c'è nulla che – rallegrandomi –
possa durare più di un frammento
più di un istante.

Ultimate bequests in a circular
gathering. Voices, syllables
ricochet through the crowd.
They come back to me:
an endless buzz from which I can only
draw a few barely fulfilling
scraps. I only feel the breathing
that accompanies the rest of my journey.

What could truly fulfill me?
Nothing that might please me
can last more than a fragment
more than an instant.

La musica è la stessa
e si ripete ossessiva come in un film.
Ricordi *Vertigo*? Ricordi quel
passo verso l'ignoto
innamorato di se stesso? Quell'ombratura
soffusa da cui scaturiva
come attraverso un velo
un'aria dolce, trasognata, infinita?
Ora quel ricordo mi accompagna
fuggendo. Dice "non ti appartengo,
non ti ho mai appartenuto."
E sono chiari e tersi
quegli occhi innamorati
quel girovagare e ritornare
sullo stesso balcone…
Ho tredici anni. Non ho che tredici anni.
Ho già tredici anni.

The music is the same
and repeats itself obsessively as in a film.
Remember *Vertigo*? Do you remember that
step toward the unknown
in love with itself? That suffused
shadow from which gushed
as if through a veil
a sweet, dreamy, infinite aria?
Now that memory accompanies me
even as it flees. It says: "I don't belong to you,
I never belonged to you".
And how clear and pure
are those lovestruck eyes
that roaming and returning
to the same balcony…
I am thirteen. I am only thirteen
I am already thirteen.

Mi volgo paziente verso gli opposti
avvenimenti. Rimando
prove impegni appuntamenti. Poco fa
ogni cosa sembrava pronta
ed è già stato tutto consumato.
Ora sono qui per raccogliere scorie
in attesa che avvampi
una qualche esplosione
la libera azione d'esprimere
ciò che posso immaginare solo
in piena indipendenza.
Come una vocazione si fa sentenza
sigillo nudo, esibito,
che sfida ogni inganno
in virtù della sua purezza
… per quell'antica luce
dorata che un tempo illuminava
il pane sulla mia tavola.

I patiently turn toward the opposite
events. I postpone
tests engagements dates. Only minutes ago
everything looked ready
and all has already been consumed.
Now I'm here to pick up the scraps
waiting for some explosion
to flare up, the free act
of expressing
what I can only imagine
in full independence.
As every vocation turns into a sentence
a naked, exhibited seal
that defies all deception
by virtue of its purity
... for the sake of that ancient light
of gold that once illuminated
the bread on my table.

Ti riguardi attonito
nell'istante che si aggiunge agli anni.
Volevi essere l'invincibile. Il primo
fra tutti. Cosa ti aspetti?
Nasce nel gruppo il sentimento
d'un giorno guerriero.
Cosa ti aspetti? Il bacio
di Anna Pierro, il desiderio
che esplode improvviso
nell'afrore estivo.
Voglio toccare la felicità
con un dito bagnato di lacrime.

You look at yourself, astonished
in the instant that adds to the years.
You wanted to be the invincible one. The first
among all. What do you expect?
The sentiment of a warlike day
is born in the group.
What do you expect? Anna Pierro's
kiss, desire exploding suddenly
in the summer heat.
I want to touch happiness
with a finger wet with tears.

Dai nostri calzoncini
sbucano ginocchia sempre sfregiate.
Il cortile raccoglie ogni giorno
voci e competizioni.
Il pallone gira impazzito, sbatte
da un muro a uno scalino.
Tutti fratelli nel sudore
che imperla la fronte. La vittoria
sta in un fuscello, in un niente,
in quel brandello supremo
di carne imbrattata di sangue.

Ever-scraped knees
pop out of our shorts.
Every day the courtyard gathers
voices and contests.
The football spins madly, bangs
from wall to step.
We are all brothers in the sweat
that beads our forehead. Victory
lies in a twig, in a trifle,
in that ultimate shred
of blood-soiled flesh.

Nelle rovine della fortuna
sono un piccolo soldato che parte
per una guerra immaginaria.
Altri mari altri continenti.
Così m'illudo di figurarmi. Così,
nel candore dei miei tredici anni.

In fortune's ruins
I am a little soldier leaving
for an imaginary war.
Different seas, different continents.
This is how I think I envision myself. This,
with the innocence of my thirteen years.

Corriamo in fila
di fronte al padre di Tonino Iannone,
giardiniere sempre un po' stupito, un po' trasognato.
In altre stanze smania
una figlia di nessuno.
Chi raccoglierà queste nude foglie?
Il tempo cambierà in fretta.
Nessuno scende più per quella
stradetta che ci conduceva a Fratte:
tutto stravolto tutto stritolato
in un subbuglio di crescita orrenda. Nulla
più riconoscibile.
Salerno, Via Parmenide 30:
cinque anni della mia adolescenza.

We run in single file
in front of Tonino Iannone's father,
gardener always a bit amazed, a bit moonstruck.
In some other room a nobody's
daughter is yearning.
Who will pick up these bare leaves?
The weather will change quickly.
Nobody ever walks anymore down that
little road that led us to Fratte:
everything torn everything crushed
in a turmoil of horrendous growth. Nothing
recognizable anymore.
Salerno, via Parmenide 30:
five years of my adolescence.

Ristabiliamo le distanze
fra ciò che è sempre stato imminente
e il vuoto che ci è accanto.
La tua voce è in quell'orlo
che corona il cratere. Un sibilo
e si disperde la polvere del giorno. Non sai
più se è ieri o domani
perché domani e ieri
sono precipitati nel nulla
e le sillabe impazzite
si confondono tra di loro.
La nostra adolescenza
resta incisa in un'espressione
un po' casuale, in un profilo sghembo,
in un gesto che non è mai nato
ma che c'è sempre stato.

Let us reestablish the distance
between what has always been imminent
and the emptiness beside us.
Your voice is in that edge
that crowns the crater. One hiss
and the day's dust is dispersed. You can't tell
tomorrow from yesterday
because yesterday and tomorrow
have fallen into nothingness
and the crazed syllables
get confused between each other.
Our adolescence
remains enshrined in a slightly
casual expression, in a crooked profile,
in a gesture that was never born
yet has always been there.

Il nostro spazio è il rustico campetto
sotto casa. Da lì gli appuntamenti
visuali, un sorriso, qualche bigliettino.
Aspetto Anna sotto il cavalcavia
di Fratte, Via Sabato de Vita.
Domattina mio padre ed io
partiremo per Roma in avanscoperta.
Lasciamo Salerno per sempre
gli altri della famiglia
ci raggiungeranno poi
com'è giusto che sia.
Ho tredici anni. Si sta facendo
tardi. Aspetto Anna sotto il cavalcavia.
Non verrà.

Our space is the rustic little field
down the street. From there the visual
appointments, a smile, a few written notes.
I wait for Anna under the Fratte
overpass, Via Sabato de Vita.
In the morning my father and I
will be off to Rome for reconnaissance.
We leave Salerno forever
the rest of the family
will join us later
as they should.
I am thirteen years old. It's getting
late. I wait for Anna under the overpass.
She won't come.

II

LA NOTTE

Mi ripiego verso la sacra notte, impronunciabile,
colma di misteri.
Novalis

II

NIGHT

Aside I turn to the holy, unspeakable,
mysterious Night.
               Novalis

La sacra notte invoca
una calma rivolta: una sirena
che chiama a raccolta i seguaci del nulla
i secondini del nostro quadrato.

A braccia in giù…
come quella prima volta di fronte
a Mont Saint-Michel. Si staglia
improvvisamente
dinanzi ai miei occhi
quel pomeriggio di tarda estate
che sembra già inverno.
Lo ricordo bene. Christiane
corre davanti a me controvento.
Io raccolgo un'alga lunga
due metri. Non c'è
nessun altro vicino a noi.
Sembra già inverno
e noi, trasparenti,
ci inerpichiamo tra i bastioni dell'abbazia,
come penitenti.

The sacred night invokes
a calm revolt: a siren
rallying the devotees of nothingness
the jailers of our section.

Slack-armed…
just like that first time in front
of Mont Saint-Michel. Suddenly
a late-summer afternoon looms up
before my eyes
that already feels like winter.
I remember it well. Christiane
is running ahead of me against the wind.
I pick up a strand of algae
two meters long. There is
no one else near us.
It already feels like winter
and we, transparent,
clamber through the abbey's bastions,
like penitents.

Talvolta la notte sorprende
chi l'attraversa. La notte
che assorbe tutto, che custodisce
o rinnova il silenzio, i giochi della mente,
incoscienze, il sangue di qualche innocente.

La sacra notte, che a tua volta sorprendi
nel suo grumo, intatta,
senza compromessi. Una storia
come immaginata, perfetta nei suoi
scismi, nei suoi effetti, nei suoi delitti.

Come quella volta –
4 febbraio 1983 - che l'attraversasti barcollando
il sangue ti colava sulla fronte
sempre di più, avanti, nel buio pesto
dalla 207 fino a 100 Park Terrace West.

A casa lo specchio ti rimandò
la tua faccia inorridita… telefonasti
a Judith meccanicamente, ti disse soltanto
di socchiudere la porta d'ingresso
prima che tu, immemore, stramazzassi a terra.

Poi altri spazi, bianchi, bianchissimi.
Tutto più leggero, tutto più soffice
come la neve che trasognato
vedevi turbinare nei fiocchi

Sometimes the night surprises
those who cross it. The all-absorbing
night, which guards or renews
the silence, the mind games,
recklessness, the blood of an innocent.

The sacred night, which you in turn surprise
in its lump, intact,
without compromises. An almost
imagined story, perfect in its
schisms, its effects, its crimes.

Like that one time –
February 4th, 1983 – you staggered through it
more and more blood dripping down
your forehead, onward, in the pitch darkness
from 207 St. to 100 Park Terrace West.

At home the mirror threw your horrified face
back at you… mechanically, you dialed
Judith's number, she only managed to tell you
to leave the entrance door ajar
before you crumpled to the floor, oblivious.

Then other white spaces, bone-white.
All lighter, all softer
like the snow you saw in your stupor
the whirl of snowflakes

che si stampavano sul parabrezza.

Ora è solo racconto, film muto, labbra
semoventi di barellieri e infermieri
le identiche domande ogni poco:
sogno e realtà nell'unica sequenza,
sempre la stessa, sempre la stessa.

È solo un racconto,
film muto che ripete la notte: questa
notte che si è data appuntamento
con un' altra di trent'anni fa.

Mount Sinai, 4 febbraio 2013

smacking against the windshield.

Now it's just storytelling, a silent film, self-moving
lips of stretcher-bearers and nurses
the identical questions at short intervals:
dream and reality within the same sequence,
always the same, always the same.

It's just a story,
a silent film that repeats the night: this
night that has made a date with another one
from thirty years ago.

Mount Sinai, February 4, 2013

Nel sonno la scena si ripete
in altre forme. Altre
le persone, altri i sentimenti, altre
le figurazioni, come quella
di appena un mese fa, a Sorrento.
Il cancello del grande albergo
a picco sul mare
era chiuso. Accompagno
una ragazza lungo il viottolo
che porta all'entrata principale...

"Qui dentro nacque Torquato Tasso".
Così, il pallido albergatore
nella sua passività contemplativa
mentre mi fornisce opuscoli e timide occhiate.
Io rividi subito in lui il Principe Myskin...
Ho vissuto quattro anni e più
fuori dalla Russia; e come ne ero partito! Quasi
non avevo la testa a segno!
Allora non sapevo niente, e adesso è anche peggio.
Ho bisogno di persone buone.

In my sleep the scene repeats itself
in different shapes. With other
people, other feelings, other
figurations, like the one
from only a month ago, in Sorrento.
The gate of the big hotel
overlooking the sea
was locked. I am escorting
a girl down the path
that leads to the main entrance...

"Torquato Tasso was born here",
said the wan hotelier
in his contemplative passivity
as he furnished me with brochures and timid glances.
At once I saw in him Prince Myshkin...
I lived more than four years
outside of Russia; and what state I was in when I left!
I was nearly out of my mind!
I didn't know anything back then, and now it's even worse.
I need good people.

Scavo ogni notte nella mia caverna
penetro nelle tacche della ruota dentata.
Pochi i benefici. Ristorare
il sorriso sulla smorfia
è un esercizio che richiede fede. Dormire,
insonnarsi d'oblio, ripetere
gesti modulazioni forme
come un inno o una preghiera
nelle sue variazioni.

... penso a un bambino appena nato alla vita
che già piange la sua non esistenza.
Come faremo, noi genitori, a farci
perdonare per avergliela data?

Every night I dig in my cave
penetrate into the teeth of the cog wheel.
Few are the benefits. Restoring
the smile on the smirk
is an exercise requiring faith. Sleeping,
stunning oneself with forgetfulness, repeating
gestures modulations forms
like a hymn or a prayer
in its variations.

…I think of a child only just born into life
and already crying over his nonexistence.
How can we, parents, ever be forgiven
for giving it to him?

Adesso nell'oscurità
tutto appare composto e fermo.
Tutto già ben disposto
ben organizzato, mentre
guardo di nuovo i miei libri allineati.
Stanotte non voleranno via
dai loro ripiani. Non permetterò
che precipitino giù, che abbandonino
il proprio abitacolo, legati
uno accanto all'altro
per puro destino alfabetico.

Now in this darkness
all appears orderly and still.
Everything well-arranged
well-organized, while
I look once more at my lined-up books.
Tonight they won't fly away
off their shelves. I won't allow them
to fall down, to abandon their abode, tied
next to each other
out of sheer alphabetical destiny.

Prima di addormentarti
lascia che i fili si facciano girandola,
lascia che un improvviso
fiocco azzurro ingravidi l'aria
a partire da quel piccolo cortile
fino a spazi imprevedibili. Lascia
che i fili si facciano girandola.

Scendono dall'alto gocciole minute.
Sono dita minuscole di mani infantili.
Nobody, not even the rain, has such small hands.
Una di esse agguanta il tuo indice.
È il suo modo di tenere
in pugno il mondo
e di aggrapparsi ad esso.

Riesci a distinguere nel luridume
la rosa desiderata
che volerà unica e silenziosa?
Vuoi distinguerti?

Facendosi largo nella ressa
tra fumi e nebbie diradanti
è apparso infine il Dissipatore:
bianco in viso, elegantemente vestito
nero il suo cappello
lieve il suo sorriso un po' beffardo.

Before you go to sleep
let the threads become a whirligig,
let a sudden
blue flake impregnate the air
starting from that little courtyard
up to unpredictable spaces. Let
the threads become a whirligig.

Minute droplets rain down from above.
They're the minuscule fingers of a child's hand.
Nobody, not even the rain, has such small hands.
One of them grabs your index finger.
It's his way of holding
the world in his grasp,
his way of holding on to it.

Can you distinguish in this filth
the coveted rose
which will fly, alone and silent?
Do you wish to distinguish yourself?

Pushing his way through the crowd
amid the fumes and the clearing fog
the Dissipator has finally appeared:
white in the face, elegantly dressed
his hat black
his smile faint and slightly mocking.

Ha teso la mano a ognuno
gli occhi socchiusi, mentre
dalla vicina montagna sgusciano
combattenti rivoluzionari. Sono
i miei alleati. Ripartirò con loro
senza voltarmi più indietro.

He holds out his hand to everyone
with narrowed eyes, while
from the nearby mountain sneak out
revolutionary fighters. They are
my allies. I will leave with them
without ever looking back.

Quanto piccolo e confuso
il nostro Centro del Mondo.
Nel dormiveglia mi sforzo di ricordarne
la primissima figurazione:
è una calda estate… dalla terrazza di mia zia
entro in cucina. Da lì passo nel soggiorno.
In fondo c'è una porta
che dà in una camera da letto.
Io arrivo appena alla maniglia…

Nella fresca penombra sento subito
l'odore dei vecchi mobili.
Mi avvicino alla sponda del letto
dove una donna
dorme – almeno credo – calma, supina.
Non ne ricordo i connotati
se non quella sua bianca
stretta mutandina che
le aderiva ai fianchi.
Con le mie minuscole dita
prendo a frugare, a raspare
ai lati così serrati. Ho quattro anni.
Voglio scardinate quelle strettoie:
continuo a raspare minuziosamente
con le mie gracili dita agli angoli…
Voglio vedere che cosa c'è sotto.
Voglio scoprire qualcosa che

How little and confused
our Center of the World.
In my half-sleep I strive to remember
its very first figuration:
It is a hot summer... from my aunt's terrace
I enter the kitchen. From there I walk
into the living room.
At the end there is a door
that opens into a bedroom.
I can barely reach the handle...

In the dim light I perceive at once
the smell of old furniture.
I draw near the edge of the bed
where a woman
is sleeping—or so I believe—calmly on her back.
I don't recall her features
except those white
tight panties of hers that
hugged her hips.
With my minuscule fingers
I start poking around, scratching
around the edges, so tightly sealed. I am four.
I want to burst those shackles:
I keep scratching at the corners
meticulously, with my scrawny fingers...
I want to see what's underneath.
I want to discover something that

oscuramente corrisponde
a un centro vitale del mondo.
Ho quattro anni e non so
il perché di quel mio impegnato lavorìo.

È il primo ricordo, la primissima
figurazione rimastami in mente.
Solo molti anni dopo
ne capirò qualche ragione
e anche quel forse tacito consenso...

obscurely corresponds
to some vital center of the world.
I am four and I don't know
the reason for my busy endeavor.

It's my first memory, the very first
figuration that has stuck in my mind.
Only many years later
would I in part understand its motivation
and also that perhaps tacit consent...

Siamo tutti e tre
in un grande letto: Anna, l'antica
e tu la presente, una
accanto all'altra, ed io
nel mezzo, in perfettissima armonia.
Stringo la mano ad ambedue
dolce e silenziosa la nostra intesa.
… ecco, rifletto sognando, sempre
così dovrebbe essere il mondo
senza astio e senza invidia.

There we are, all three of us
in a huge bed: the old Anna
and you, the new one,
next to each other, and I
in the middle, in the most perfect harmony.
I hold the hands of both
in sweet, quiet understanding.
… there, I ponder in my dream, this is how
the world should always be
without bitterness or envy.

Non estendere oltre la pazienza.
Fili di cotone i giorni che s'avvolgono.
Fare velo a questa distanza, a questo vortice.
Il falso perdono si stampa sui visi
nemici. Quanto goffi e grotteschi
in questa febbre di potere
sul proprio carrozzone
i detentori della nostra pubblica res.

Do not extend your patience any further.
The days curl up like cotton threads.
We must cloak this distance, this vortex.
False forgiveness imprints itself on enemy
faces. In this fever for power
how clumsy and grotesque
on their circus wagon
the keepers of our *res publica*.

Procedo in un sentiero ambiguo
per fiammate improvvise
senza verità
ma con la passione del momento,
e scoprendo a volte nello sguardo di un altro
una fede perduta....

                              Nel sogno
osservo una coppietta in un treno che
va dalla città alla periferia.
Sono rimasti sempre più soli.
I compagni di viaggio
sono scesi alle stazioni precedenti.
In questo vagone, immobili nel tempo,
ora appaiono tutti quelli che ho amato.

I proceed down an ambiguous path
by sudden bursts of flame
without truth
but with the passion of the moment,
at times discovering a lost faith
in someone else's gaze...

                                      In my dream
I observe a young couple on a train headed
from the city to the suburbs...
They've been left more and more alone.
Their traveling companions
have all gotten off at previous stops.
In this car, motionless in time,
appear now all the people I've loved.

Un mio compagno di viaggio
si fa chiamare in altro modo.
Vuole essere
quello che di noi due ama di più.
Nello scintillare degli occhi
c'è il concentrato istantaneo
della sua piccola storia. Altri
verranno da lui.
Altri gli chiederanno compagnia.
Inutile farsi vedere invincibili.
Siamo e restiamo solo iniziali
e il nostro corpo sa adattarsi presto.

A fellow traveler of mine
prefers to be called a different name.
Of the two of us, he wants to be
the more loving one.
In the glint of his eyes
is the instant concentrate
of his little story. Others
will come to him.
Others will ask for his companionship.
It is pointless to want to look invincible.
We are and will remain only initials
and our bodies can adapt quickly.

Calmi e impettiti
mi aspettano i libri
compagni di ogni notte
vigili sempre più sbiaditi.
Davanti alla porta chiusa
bruciano le mie e le loro storie
scacchi risentimenti ambizioni
memorie. Ora guardami di spalle.
Riconoscimi, Notte.
Avvolgimi.
Diventiamo un solo colore.

Calm and erect
my books await me
my every night's companions
ever-fading sentinels.
In front of the closed door
their stories and mine burn on:
defeats resentments ambitions
memories. Now look at me from behind.
Recognize me, o Night.
Cover me.
Let us become one color.

Solo esercizi muti
ripetizioni che non sono
uguali a se stesse. Un imbonitore
invisibile ha tracciato la strada.
Le sue mani
mischiano ininterrottamente
un mazzo di carte sgualcito, mentre
un volto va scomparendo nel gorgo.
Quanto minuscolo e confuso
il nostro centro! Soltanto
esercizi muti, labbra
che mimano parole asonore
ripetizioni
ripetizioni…
Morte Notte, cancella ogni rumore
e della mente ogni dolore.

Only mute exercises
repetitions that aren't
identical with themselves. An invisible
charlatan has laid out the path.
His hands
incessantly shuffle
a worn-out deck of cards, as a face
disappears into the whirlpool.
How minuscule and confused
is our center! Only
mute exercises, lips
miming soundless words
repetitions
repetitions...
O Death Night, cancel all noise
and all the pain in my mind.

Notte catabasi,
Notte,
vieni,
rovinami addosso.
Rianima il sabba
i miei oggi
i miei ieri.
Sillabe ricontate
voci contorte
sussurri
volti invocati.
Sorella Notte,
Madre Notte:
Notte mente e niente
di tutti i miei pensieri.

O Night katabasis
o Night,
come,
crumble all over me.
Resurrect the sabbath
my todays
my yesterdays.
Recounted syllables
twisted voices
whispers
conjured faces.
Sister Night,
Mother Night:
Night mind and nothingness
of all my thoughts.

La Notte stanotte è una lieve ballerina
un minuscolo pellicano che
vola tra bianchi vapori
porta nel becco, come in un lampo,
la mia giovinezza... un filo d'erba -
ora improvvisamente ricordo -
un filo d'erba
fu il primo regalo di Emma.

Tonight the Night is a lithe ballerina
a tiny pelican that
flies amid white vapors
carrying in its beak, as in a flash,
my youth… a blade of grass—
now I suddenly remember—
a blade of grass
was Emma's first gift.

Acquetarsi infine
sottrarsi almeno per un breve intervallo
da ogni male, libero volare
assottigliarsi gradualmente
fino a svanire nel buio, essere
tu il buio, il buio assoluto.

To quieten, at last
to shun at least for a brief interval
all that is evil, to fly free
to wear thinner and thinner
until you disperse in the darkness, for you
to be darkness, absolute darkness.

Nati per ardere e morire
ad ogni istante. Affrontiamo
spavaldi il nemico. Rivedo
il pugno sul viso di chi ha offeso
il mio compagno di banco Aldo Stella.
Impietrito nello scatto automatico ed eterno.
Il sangue che d'improvviso riga la mia mano.

Ci saranno altri giorni. Altre
partite altre scale
da discendere sempre
più in fretta, volando
sul corrimano... palla da bigliardo
che sbatte impazzita
e precisa di sponda in sponda.

We were born to burn and die
at every instant. Brashly
we face the enemy. I see again
the fist to the face of the offender
of my seatmate Aldo Stella.
Frozen in the automatic, eternal snapshot.
Blood suddenly streaking my hand.

There will be more days. More
games more stairs
to descend faster
and faster, flying
down the banister... a billiard ball
bouncing from cushion to cushion
crazed and precise.

Cadono i birilli prima del tempo
dentro i miei occhi. Ragazzi
scommettono sui minuti
nella brace di una sigaretta.
Ragazzi destinati alla divisione.
Ragazzi che tra poco
non sapranno più riconoscersi.

The bowling pins fall prematurely
into my eyes. Boys
wager on the minutes
in a cigarette's ashes.
Boys destined for separation.
Boys who in a little while
won't know each other anymore.

Ciò che ci appartiene veramente
non ritornerà mai più. Il freddo
stanotte consuma le ossa e
lascia i vivi senza compagnia.
Frughi nel dormiveglia ripensando ad altro…
Rivedi l'Irno oggi inaridito
ridotto a un rigagnolo tra sassi e sterpi
al centro della tua vecchia città
oggi ricreata in bellezza.
È un giorno qualunque
come tanti altri.
I ragazzi a piazza San Francesco
si ammassano davanti al Tasso.
Qualcuno di soppiatto
ti slaccia l'elastico dei libri…
volano nell'aria tra urla e sghignazzi.
Volano i quaderni, vola il tuo basco nuovo,
stropicciato in mani estranee. Rivedi
i tuoi falsi compagni
che inveiscono attorno a te…
i loro volti fermi, ora, come fossero di pietra,
uno per uno immobili. Rivedi i riccioli di Berto
disteso per terra. Rivedi il tuo cielo
e quei tuoi assurdi pantalonetti alla zuava
improvvisamente chiazzati di fango e sangue.

Sono andati tutti via. È un giorno qualunque

What truly belongs to us
will never return. Tonight
the cold eats away at the bones
leaving the living without company.
You rummage in your half-sleep pondering other
things...
You see the Irno river again, now all dried up
into a trickle between snakes and stones
in the heart of your old city
now recreated in beauty.
It's an ordinary day
like many others.
The boys in piazza San Francesco
flock in front of Tasso.
Somebody stealthily
unties the string around your books...
they fly up in the air amid screams and laughter.
Your notebooks fly, and your new beret as well,
rumpled by stranger hands. You see again
your false friends
sounding off all around you...
their faces inert, now, as if made of stone,
one by one, motionless. You see Berto's curls
as he lies on the ground. You see your sky
and those ridiculous knickerbockers
suddenly stained with mud and blood.

They are all gone. It is an ordinary day

come tanti altri, questo
che ti vede lentamente
raccattare libri e quaderni, fogli impantanati
insieme all'inerte berretto.

Allora ti dirai che sei davvero nato. Ti dirai che
forse è davvero tutto governato dal Caso.

Ti dirai come si fa a perdere gli altri
come si fa a guadagnare se stessi.

like many others, this day
that sees you slowly
picking up books and notebooks, muddied sheets
along with that lifeless beret.

Then you will tell yourself that you were really born.
You will tell yourself that perhaps all is ruled by
Chance.

You will tell yourself how you can lose the others
how you can gain yourself.

Che sia ora così: tutto andato
tutto triturato. Ecco Via del Carmine
che faccio ogni mattina da Fratte
a Piazza San Francesco. Che sia tutto
benedetto in questo fermo mattino
in questo fumo demente e dimentico
un istante, questo, che ci vede in fila.

Parlo di nuovo con un compagno
col quale condivido il banco:
Aldo Stella, confinato
nei riccioli di un pallido
sorriso. Io voglio essere te, Aldo.
Un giorno io ti piangerò.

La memoria è questo ragazzo.
Ingoia chitarre e sogni proibiti.
L'estate a Salerno è lunga
un eterno martirio. Certi pomeriggi
baci rubati in un minuscolo androne
abbracciato a una ragazza
che va perdendo le sue dita.

Tutto torna in giusta misura
la tavola apparecchiata... gli occhi
spiritati di mio padre. Tutto
si bilancia nell'ardore di qualche scoperta.
Volti anonimi

Let it be thus, then: all gone
all ground up. Here is Via del Carmine
that I take every day from Fratte
to piazza San Francesco. Let it all be
blessed in this still morning
in this demented, forgetful smoke
this instant that sees us in single file.

I'm again talking to the friend
with whom I share a desk:
Aldo Stella, confined
within the curls of a pale
smile. I want to be you, Aldo.
Someday I will mourn you.

Memory is this boy.
It swallows guitars and forbidden dreams.
It is a long summer in Salerno
an eternal martyrdom. Some afternoons
stolen kisses in a tiny entrance hall
as I cling to a girl
who is losing her fingers.

Everything comes back in the right measure
the set table... my father's
wild eyes. Everything
balances out in the ardor of some discovery.
Anonymous faces

che aspirano a farsi maschere. Lotto
con l'oscurità del tempo.
Rimetto in ballo qualche scommessa.

C'erano i miei amici:
uno spargimento di richiami e architravi.
Lotte senza quartiere. Tutto si bilancia.
Tutto si disvela.
Anche il più vile può essere un eroe.

aspiring to become masks. I struggle
with time's obscurity.
I take up betting again.

There were my friends:
a spread of signals and lintels.
Fights without quarter. Everything balances out.
Everything is unveiled.
Even the most craven can be heroes.

Capita sempre un momento in cui
a un tratto saetta un richiamo
esatto. Un semplice comando e
la luce sembra magicamente disfarsi
nella tua camera da letto.
È notte.
Una medaglia luminosa
unifica i pari di grado
quelli che si riconoscono
in un unico stemma.
Ma adesso è già tardi. Tutto
si attutisce, e tu frughi
negli anfratti delle pause
quando si pretende d'essere vivi
e ogni gesto può essere ultimo
e primo.

A moment always arrives when
there suddenly flits
an exact signal. A simple command and
the light appears magically to unravel
in your bedroom.
It is nighttime.
A bright medal
unifies those equal in rank
those who recognize themselves
in the same emblem.
But now it's already too late. Everything
becomes muffled, and you rifle
through the pauses' nooks and crannies
when we claim to be alive
and every gesture could be our last
and first.

Una sfida di farfalla, libera vibra.
Cosa mi suggerisce? Unica
invenzione. Una sapienza infinita.
Ogni notte porta il proprio destino.
Ogni notte allarga le braccia. Misteriosa
e docile nei suoi richiami.
Notte lunga e impietosa. Porta
là dove si rivela il passaggio fra amore
e disamore, ingenuità e scaltrezza...
con la coscienza della sua finzione.

The challenge of a butterfly vibrating freely.
What does it suggest to me? A unique
invention. An infinite wisdom.
Every night brings its own destiny.
Every night spreads its arms. Mysterious
and docile in its signals.
Long and merciless night. It carries you
where the passage is revealed between love
and disaffection, naivety and shrewdness…
with the awareness of its masquerade.

Scorre questa notte primitiva, senza minuti e senza monumenti. Cadono birilli a volontà. Il tempo ruba tempo, con lo scatto degli occhi, pronti a svelare ogni finzione. Non riesci a capire il suo nodo... come quando un istante si scioglie sul filo di lana e il vincitore taglia il traguardo sotto la folla ammassata sugli spalti. Basterebbe un nonnulla a scardinare quello sventolio di bandierine e di braccia. Un silenzio secolare già avvolgerebbe le loro sagome ferme, come di pietra, le maschere incollate per sempre sui visi. Scorre questa notte primitiva, senza minuti e senza monumenti. E ogni ombra si ricompatta nel suo stampo.

È nella nostra debolezza
che risiede la nostra
immortale umanità.
Ma chi, in realtà, vorrebbe
essere immortale? I giorni
si susseguono ai giorni
e le notti alle notti.
Un maleficio circolare:
libero e puntuale. Chi
vorrebbe davvero essere immortale?

This primitive night wears on, without minutes or monuments. Bowling pins are falling left and right. Time steals time, with the dart of eyes ready to unveil every pretense. You can't understand its knot… as when an instant melts away on the woolen thread and the winner crosses the finish line under the crowd massed in the bleachers. It would take but a trifle to unhinge that waving of flags and arms. A centuries-old silence would already be enshrouding their silhouettes, motionless like stone, masks forever glued to their faces. This primitive night wears on, without minutes or monuments. And each shadow is reassembled once more in its mold.

It is in our weakness
that our immortal
humanity resides.
But who, really, would wish
to be immortal? The days
follow one another, and so
do the nights. A circular
evil spell: free and punctual. Who
would really wish to be immortal?

O felice incoscienza dei ragazzi!
Nella primavera che s'annuncia crudele
c'è il destino di ogni consanguineo.
Cercare nella mano di un altro
il fiato che ci ruba la distanza.

Comincia così ogni conoscenza
che anticipa nel rogo la sua fine.
Che cosa chiedere agli innamorati?
Che cosa chiedere se non la dimenticanza
del proprio esser vivi e trasparenti?

Amici,
noi siamo già passati di qui.
Vibra nella notte l'anima del mondo.
Si distaccano dalla parete mobile
gli spettri dei corpi che fummo.
Che cosa chiedere agli innamorati?
Furiosamente gira su se stessa
quella parete circolare, creature appiattite
su cui, a tratti, scivolano
fasci di luce balenanti.
Vietato parlare. Vietato scrivere.

O carefree recklessness of the young!
In this spring shaping up to be cruel
lies the fate of every kin.
To seek in another's hand
the breath that robs us of distance.

So begins every knowledge
that envisions its end at the stake.
What should we ask of lovers?
What should we ask but that they forget
their being alive and transparent?

Friends,
we have already passed through here.
The soul of the world vibrates in the night.
From the movable wall break off
the ghosts of the bodies we were.
What should we ask of lovers?
How furiously that circular wall revolves,
flattened creatures on which, at times
glide flashing beams of light.
All talking forbidden. All writing forbidden.

NOTA

Questo libro, per il quale nel 2015 ho avuto la gioia di ricevere il Premio "Pascoli" e il Premio "Viareggio-Giuria" contiene poesie scritte dal novembre 2012 al novembre 2013. Ringrazio la casa editrice Passigli di Firenze per avermi concesso l'autorizzazione di pubblicarlo in lingua francese (traduzione di Philippe Démeron, Éditions RAZ, 2017), e ora in lingua inglese, grazie a questa fine traduzione di Giorgio Mobili.

Il libro è diviso in due sezioni che ritengo antitetiche e complementari.

La prima sezione, dedicata idealmente a François Truffaut, contiene sedici testi che sono stati anticipati nell'Almanacco di Poesia *Quadernario. Ventisette poeti d'oggi*, a cura di Maurizio Cucchi (LietoColle, 2013). I nomi citati appartengono a compagni reali della mia adolescenza, che risale al periodo in cui sono vissuto a Vietri e a Salerno fino al 1957, anno in cui la mia famiglia si trasferì a Roma. Un'adolescenza precocissima, la mia, vissuta in modo febbrile e disincantato allo stesso tempo.

In questa prima sezione inserisco anche, con alcune modifiche, due poesie, aventi rispettivamente per capoverso "Si preparava la scenografia" e "Mi volgo paziente verso gli opposti", che originariamente erano contenute nella raccolta *Disunita ombra* (Archinto, RCS, 2013).

AUTHOR'S NOTE

This book, for which I had the honor of receiving the Pascoli Prize and the Viareggio Jury Prize in 2015, contains poems written between November 2012 and April 2013. I am grateful to the Passigli Publishing House in Florence, Italy, for granting permission to publish it in French (translated by Philippe Démeron, Éditions RAZ, 2017), and now in English, thanks to this fine translation by Giorgio Mobili.

The book is divided in two sections that are both antithetical and complementary.

The first section, ideally dedicated to François Truffaut, contains sixteen poems that have previously appeared in the Poetry Almanac *Quadernario, Ventisette poeti d'oggi*, edited by Maurizio Cucchi (LietoColle, 2013). The names therein mentioned are those of real friends from my teenage years, which I spent in Vietri and Salerno until 1957, when my family moved to Rome. Mine was a very precocious adolescence, lived in a manner both feverish and disenchanted.

I have included in this section, with minor modifications, two poems beginning respectively "The choreography of the future" and "I patiently turn toward the opposite", which were originally contained in my collection *Disunita ombra* (Archinto, RCS, 2013).

La poesia che ha come capoverso "La stanza è bianchissima" è nata da una suggestione intertestuale collocabile nell'ultimo capitolo della *Coscienza di Zeno* di Italo Svevo. E, ancora a una riflessione di Svevo, sono riconducibili gli ultimi due versi della poesia che ha come capoverso "Scavo ogni notte nella mia caverna".

Gli ultimi due versi della poesia che ha come capoverso "Ti riguardi attonito" sono tratti da *Nadja* di André Breton.

La seconda sezione raccoglie testi notturni, (tra)scritti, perlopiù, in stati di dormiveglia e in momenti semi-onirici o ipnagogici. È una sezione in parte ispirata da alcune suggestioni di lettura degli *Inni alla notte* di Novalis, un poeta e prosatore che è stato determinante per la mia formazione letteraria.

Gli ultimi cinque versi della poesia che ha come capoverso "Nel sonno la scena si ripete" sono tratti da *L'idiota* di Fëdor Dostoevskij.

Il decimo verso della poesia intitolata "Prima di addormentarti" è di E.E. Cummings. In questa stessa poesia la figura del "Dissipatore" allude a un personaggio fantasmatico del racconto *Settimana di sole* di Tommaso Landolfi; racconto, a mio avviso, tra i più straordinari e avvincenti del Novecento italiano.

The poem that begins "The room is bone-white…" was born of an intertextual suggestion from the last chapter of *La coscienza di Zeno* by Italo Svevo. I am also indebted to a reflection of Svevo's for the last two lines of the poem that begins "Every night I dig in my cave".

The last two lines of the poem that begins "You look at yourself, astonished" are taken from *Nadja* by André Breton.

The second section comprises nocturnal texts, written (or transcribed) mostly in a state of half-sleep and in semi-oneiric, hypnagogic moments. It is inspired by *Hymns to the Night* by the German poet Novalis, a crucial influence in my literary formation.

The last five lines of the poem that begins "In my sleep the scene repeats itself" are taken from *The Idiot* by Fyodor Dostoyevsky.

Line 10 of poem "Before you go to sleep" is by e. e. cummings. In this same poem, the "Dissipator" alludes to a fantasmatic character from the short story *Settimana di sole* by Tommaso Landolfi, to my mind one of the most extraordinary Italian short stories of the twentieth century.

Nota sull'autore

Luigi Fontanella vive tra New York e Firenze. Ha pubblicato libri di poesia, narrativa e saggistica. Fra i titoli più recenti: *L'angelo della neve. Poesie di viaggio* (Mondadori, Almanacco dello Specchio, 2009), *Controfigura* (romanzo, Marsilio, 2009), *Migrating Words* (Bordighera Press, 2012), *Bertgang* (Moretti & Vitali, 2012, Premio Prata, Premio I Murazzi), *Disunita ombra* (Archinto, RCS, 2013). Dirige, per la casa editrice Olschki , "Gradiva", rivista internazionale di poesia e poetologia italiana (Premio per la Traduzione, Ministero dei Beni Culturali) e presiede la IPA (Italian Poetry in America).
luigi.fontanella@stonybrook.edu

About the Author

Luigi Fontanella is a poet, literary critic, novelist and translator. John S. Toll Professor of Italian at Stony Brook University, he has published numerous books of poetry, several books of fiction, and others of literary criticism. His publications include *Il surrealismo italiano* (Roma: Bulzoni, 1983); *La parola aleatoria* (Firenze: Le Lettere,1992); *Storia di Bontempelli* (Ravenna: Longo, 1997) and *Migrating Words. Italian Writers in the United States* (New York: Bordighera Press, 2012). His novels *Controfigura* (Venezia: Marsilio, 2009) and *Il dio di New York* (Firenze: Passigli, 2015). His most recent collections of poetry are *L'azzurra memoria* (Bergamo: Moretti & Vitali, 2007, Laurentum Prize); *L'angelo della neve* (Milano: Mondadori, 2009); *Disunita ombra* (Milano: Archinto-Rizzoli, 2013, Frascati Prize); *L'adolescenza e la notte* (Firenze: Passigli, 2015, Pascoli Prize, Viareggio-Giuria Prize); and *Monte Stella* (Firenze: Passigli, 2020). His poetry has been translated into French, Spanish, English and Russian. President of I.P.A. (Italian Poetry in America), Fontanella is the Senior Editor of the international journal *Gradiva*, and Chief Editor of the publishing house Gradiva Publications. He lives in Mount Sinai, Long Island, NY, and spends part of the year in Florence, Italy.

Nota sul traduttore

Giorgio Mobili (Milano, 1973) è un poeta, traduttore e critico letterario italiano residente a Fresno, in California. È autore di vari saggi e dello studio *Irritable Bodies and Postmodern Subjects in Pynchon, Puig, Volponi* (Peter Lang, 2008). La sua poesia è apparsa in svariate riviste letterarie (tra cui *L'immaginazione*, *Poesia*, *Steve*, *Gradiva*, *La Clessidra*, *Fili d'aquilone*) e nell'antologia bilingue *Poets of the Italian Diaspora* (a cura di Joseph Perricone e Luigi Bonaffini, Fordham UP, 2013). Ha pubblicato cinque raccolte poetiche: *Penelope su Sunset Boulevard* (Manni, 2010), *Planet Maruschka* (La Vita Felice, 2013), *Waterloo riconquistata* (Puntoacapo, 2014), *Miracoli ed effetti* (Pèquod, 2016), e *Dimenticare un Hotel* (Puntoacapo, 2020). Al 2013 risale la sua prima raccolta in lingua spagnola, Última salida a Ventura (Mago Editores, Santiago, Cile). Ha tradotto in italiano il poeta brasiliano Narlan Matos (*La provincia oscura*, Fili, 2016), il poeta americano Christopher Merrill (*Necessità*, Fili, 2017), e i poeti cileni Ennio Moltedo (*Ruta silenciosa*, Ediciones Vertiente, Cile, uscita prevista nel 2021) e Carmen Berenguer (*Orme di secolo*, Fili, uscita prevista 2021).

About the Translator

A translator, poet, and critic, Giorgio Mobili was born in Milan, Italy, in 1973. He has a Ph.D. in Comparative Literature from Washington University, St. Louis (MO). He currently teaches at California State University, Fresno. He is the author of several academic essays on (Post)modern literature and film, and of the book *Irritable Bodies and Postmodern Subjects in Pynchon, Puig, and Volponi* (Peter Lang, 2008). His Italian poetry has appeared in several journals, five published collections (starting with *Penelope su Sunset Boulevard*, Manni, 2010), and has been included in the bilingual anthology *Poets of the Italian Diaspora* (Fordham UP, 2013). His first Spanish book (*Última salida a Ventura*, Mago, 2013) came out in Santiago, Chile. His English poetry has appeared in *The Tipton Poetry Journal*, *Pank Magazine*, The *Hiram Poetry Review*, *Ariel*, and *Gradiva*. He has translated, for the first time into Italian, the Brazilian poet Narlan Matos (*La provincia oscura*, Fili, 2016), the American poet Christopher Merrill (*Necessità*, Fili, 2017), and the Chilean poets Ennio Moltedo (*Ruta silenciosa*, forthcoming in 2021) and Carmen Berenguer (*Orme di secolo*, forthcoming in 2021).

Other books by Luigi Fontanella available in English:

From G. to G. (New York: Peter Lang, 1996, with Giose Rimanelli), translated from the Italian by Luigi Bonaffini and others.

Hot Dog, a novel (Lewinston, NY: Soleil, 1998), translated from the Italian by Justin Vitiello.

The Transparent Life and Other Poems (Stony Brook, NY: Gradiva Publications, 2000), translated from the Italian by Michael Palma

Angels of Youth (Las Cruces, New Mexico: Xenos Books, 2000), Translated from the Italian by Carol Lettieri and Irene Marchegiani.

Land of Time. Selected Poems 1972-2003 (New York: Chelsea Editions, 2006), edited by Irene Marchegiani.

Fomite

More poetry and dual language books from Fomite...

Poetry
Anna Blackmer — *Hexagrams*
L. Brown — *Loopholes*
Sue D. Burton — *Little Steel*
David Cavanagh — *Cycling in Plato's Cave*
James Connolly — *Picking Up the Bodies*
Greg Delanty — *Loosestrife*
Mason Drukman — *Drawing on Life*
J. C. Ellefson — *Foreign Tales of Exemplum and Woe*
Tina Escaja/Mark Eisner — *Caida Libre/Free Fall*
Anna Faktorovich — *Improvisational Arguments*
Barry Goldensohn — *Snake in the Spine, Wolf in the Heart*
Barry Goldensohn — *The Hundred Yard Dash Man*
Barry Goldensohn — *The Listener Aspires to the Condition of Music*
R. L. Green — *When You Remember Deir Yassin*
Gail Holst-Warhaft — *Lucky Country*
Raymond Luczak — *A Babble of Objects*
Kate Magill — *Roadworthy Creature, Roadworthy Craft*
Tony Magistrale — *Entanglements*
Gary Mesick — *General Discharge*
Andreas Nolte — *Mascha: The Poems of Mascha Kaléko*
Sherry Olson — *Four-Way Stop*
Brett Ortler — *Lessons of the Dead*
David Polk — *Drinking the River*
Janice Miller Potter — *Meanwell*
Janice Miller Potter — *Thoreau's Umbrella*
Philip Ramp — *The Melancholy of a Life as the Joy of Living It Slowly Chills*
Joseph D. Reich — *A Case Study of Werewolves*
Joseph D. Reich — *Connecting the Dots to Shangrila*
Joseph D. Reich — *The Derivation of Cowboys and Indians*
Joseph D. Reich — *The Hole That Runs Through Utopia*
Joseph D. Reich — *The Housing Market*
Kenneth Rosen and Richard Wilson — *Gomorrah*
Fred Rosenblum — *Playing Chicken with an Iron Horse*
Fred Rosenblum — *Vietnumb* \
David Schein — *My Murder and Other Local News*
Lawrence Schimel — *Desert Memory: Poems of Jeannette L. Clariond*

Fomite

Harold Schweizer — *Miriam's Book*
Scott T. Starbuck — *Carbonfish Blues*
Scott T. Starbuck — *Hawk on Wire*
Scott T. Starbuck — *Industrial Oz*
Seth Steinzor — *Among the Lost*
Seth Steinzor — *To Join the Lost*
Susan Thomas — *In the Sadness Museum*
Susan Thomas — *The Empty Notebook Interrogates Itself*
Sharon Webster — *Everyone Lives Here*
Tony Whedon — *The Tres Riches Heures*
Tony Whedon — *The Falkland Quartet*
Claire Zoghb — *Dispatches from Everest*

Poetry - Dual Language
Vito Bonito/Alison Grimaldi Donahue — *Soffiata Via/Blown Away*
Antonello Borra/Blossom Kirschenbaum — *Alfabestiario*
Antonello Borra/Blossom Kirschenbaum — *AlphaBetaBestiaro*
Antonello Borra/Anis Memon — *Fabbrica delle idee/The Factory of Ideas*
Aristea Papalexandrou/Philip Ramp — *Μας προσπερνά/It's Overtaking Us*
Mikis Theodoraksi/Gail Holst-Warhaft — *The House with the Scorpions*
Paolo Valesio/Todd Portnowitz — *La Mezzanotte di Spoleto/Midnight in Spoleto*

For more information or to order any of our books, visit:
http://www.fomitepress.com/our-books.html

Writing a review on Amazon, Good Reads, Shelfari, Library Thing or other social media sites for readers will help the progress of independent publishing. To submit a review, go to the book page on any of the sites and follow the links for reviews. Books from independent presses rely on reader-to-reader communications.

www.ingramcontent.com/pod-product-compliance
Lightning Source LLC
Chambersburg PA
CBHW021426070526
44577CB00001B/83